Rare and Unusual Creatures

T0337797

Contents

Written by Abbie Rushton

Collins

Hello from Tamsyn

My name is Tamsyn. I'm in a group called The Pioneers. I'm on a mission to earn my top spotter badge! I'm going to spot some very special creatures. They are unusual – some are quite strange!

Reptiles and frogs
Purple frog

This frog spends most of its life underground. In fact, it's in the dark so much, it's a bit of a mystery to scientists!

small eyes

long snout

short limbs

Glass frog

This is not a typical frog because you can peer inside it! You can even watch food going through its gut.

Interesting!

Mata mata

This turtle's gnarly back helps it hide in leaves, so it can sneak up on its **prey**.

Mammals

Star-nosed mole

The star-nosed mole has poor vision. It relies on touch and vibrations to find food.

Fun fact

This mole is the world's fastest eater!

Platypus

A platypus looks like a mixture of a duck, a beaver and an otter. Males can be vicious: don't disturb them! They may plunge their venomous spur into you, which would cause severe pain.

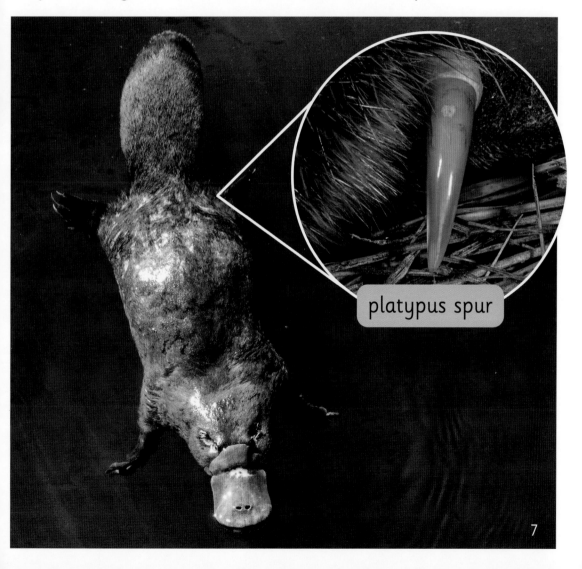

platypus spur

Lowland streaked tenrec

The tenrec looks like a hedgehog crossed with a shrew. When they are threatened, their spikes go straight up to defend themselves. They can also rub their spikes together to make a high-pitched clicking sound to communicate with each other.

Mouse deer

Despite its name, this creature isn't a deer ... or a mouse! It's more closely related to a camel, but it's about the size of a rabbit.

This one wins for sheer cuteness!

Sea animals

Leafy seadragon

If you think this is just some seaweed, look again!
Leafy seadragons are amazing at hiding.

Fun fact

Seahorses and seadragons
are the only known **species**
where the males get pregnant.

Red-lipped batfish

Apart from their stern appearance, there is something else that is fascinating about this fish. They use their fins like legs to walk on the seabed!

Wobbegong

This may look like a carpet, but can you see its tail? It's actually a shark. The wobbegong waits patiently on the seabed then uses its large mouth to snap up food swimming past.

Sea pig

These animals have toxins in their skin. This makes them taste strange to **predators**. They live in the depths of the sea, where there is not much protection for creatures like baby crabs. So the baby crabs climb onto the sea pigs to hide!

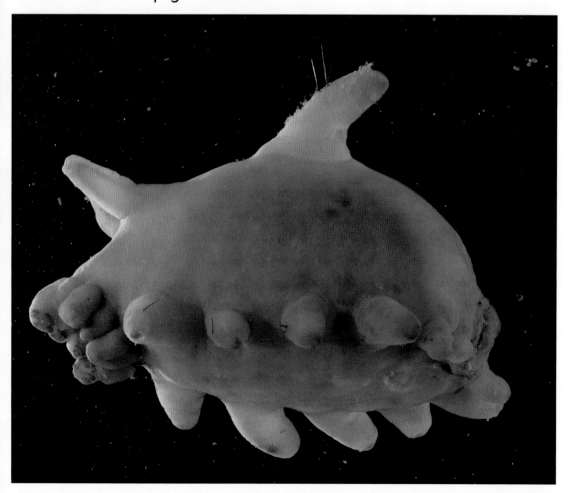

Birds

Potoo

These **nocturnal** birds get their name from their eerie cry, which sounds like *po-too*! Their wide eyes give them great night vision for hunting.

Umbrellabird

The male umbrellabird performs two tricks designed to get the attention of a mate:

1. The crest on his head fans out like an umbrella.

2. The pouch on his throat (wattle) inflates.

crest

wattle

Insects and spiders

Peacock spider

Male peacock spiders dance to show off their bright backs to females. If the male fails to make a good impression, the ferocious female will eat him!

Panda ant

It's not a panda ... or an ant! This creature is a wasp.
The females are wingless but the males are known
to fly.

Rosy maple moth

Some creatures are good at blending in. This rosy maple moth is not one of them! Experts think that its bright colours are designed to trick birds into thinking it is not nice to eat.

Great! It's time for a celebration! You helped me earn my top spotter badge. Even better, you deserve one too! Congratulations!

Glossary

nocturnal awake at night

predators animals that hunt others

prey animal that's eaten by other animals

species a group of living things
  that can breed

Index

Unusual creatures

🐾 Review: After reading 🐾

Use your assessment from hearing the children read to choose any GPCs, words or tricky words that need additional practice.

Read 1: Decoding

- Ask the children to read the following to practise focus phonemes /j/ dge ge, /m/ mb /i/ y /ai/ ea /sh/ ti.

  hedgehog   **strange**   **limbs**   **typical**   **great**   **celebration**

- Point to the speech bubbles on pages 4 and 9 in turn. Challenge the children to read them fluently as speech. Say: Try to blend in your head when you read these words.

Read 2: Prosody

- Model reading the text on pages 16 and 17 to the children as if you are a television presenter.
- Afterwards, point out how you used emphasis, pace and a changing tone to make the meaning clear for listeners.
- Challenge children to choose another page and read it as if they were a television presenter.

Read 3: Comprehension

- Ask the children whether they have seen any of the creatures, or similar creatures. Where did they see them? What did they learn about them?
- Discuss the title and the difference between the words **Rare** and **Unusual**. Ask: Can a creature be both rare and unusual? Point out how it's possible that all the creatures in the book might be both.
- On page 7, point to the word **plunge**. Ask: Could the author have used "put" instead? Discuss the context and how **plunge** is more specific and covers the sudden downward movement of the spike.
- Discuss whether certain words are technical, or whether they can be swapped for a word/phrase with a similar meaning.
  - Point to the word **fins** on page 11. Ask: Could we swap this for "legs"? Discuss how fins is a scientific term, and can't be changed to "legs".
  - Point to **carpet** on page 12. Ask: Could we swap this for "rug"? (*yes, because **carpet** is being used to describe, not name*)
  - Point to **panda** in the heading on page 17. Ask: Can we swap this for "striped"? (*we could but then we would be describing it, and not giving it its proper, scientific name*)
- Look together at pages 22 and 23. Can the children identify the animals shown? How many names and facts can they remember? Which animal did they find most interesting, and why?